UNWRI

'This collection comes at you like a lantern from the shadows. With a creak of the floorboards and wash of delight, Hannah Lavery has brought something gothic and gorgeous to life in these pages'

WILLIAM LETFORD

'Gloriously unrelenting in its ferocity for life, and righteously rallying in its deftness of consequence. This book is galvanic, gallus, gritty and gallant aw at once. Never without its theatre, never without its thrum, through the tenderness it thrashes. As brilliantly bifurcated as Edina itself: from hauntingly elegiac to sharply tender; from deftly sparing to triumphantly trenchant – this collection thrills, throbs and soars in muckle measures'

MICHAEL PEDERSEN

'Part a love letter to her lost father; part homage to the silent women in Stevenson's *Jekyll and Hyde*, Hannah Lavery's *Unwritten Woman* is a great broth of a book. A nod to Ntozake Shange with the haar coming in from the sea, Lavery takes us on a new uncharted journey. Tender and fierce. Hers is a voice to reckon with!'

JACKIE KAY

'*Unwritten Woman* is a shock of poetry, a propellant collection, that forces us to explore what skin means, what body becomes, what the place of woman is both historically and in a contemporary context. It is one woman alone in a dark room with a torch. Delicate and furious, *Unwritten Woman* is an instant feminist classic, and a collection that should be on every young woman's bookshelf, and beyond. It announces Lavery as a thinker of width, nuance, and challenge, asking the questions that might help us answer to ourselves. Outstanding'

JOELLE TAYLOR

'*Unwritten Woman* is an exquisite collection that highlights Hannah Lavery's masterful skills with narrative and form. Lavery's skilful hand as a playwright adds thrilling dimension to these poems, and she crafts scenes that are imbued with a stunning poetics'

ALYCIA PIRMOHAMED

'I loved reading this collection. Hannah's poems give me the best sort of shivers; this was incredible. The best poetry books for me allow the most wonderfully wrought and writhing insight into other worlds, minds and memories; this did that in so many extraordinarily written ways. This book is a wonder; like sitting in a roomful of flickering midnight candles gazing into the most vivid of flames; utterly illuminating. Extraordinary! Thank goodness for Hannah Lavery'

HOLLIE MCNISH

'Hannah Lavery is a resurrection woman, poet of genius, citizen of an unseen city, chronicler of hard times and enduring love, a conduit for rarely heard voices. *Unwritten Woman* is an extraordinary collection, absences revealed through erasure and attention to what is truly there. These poems are worthy of their source material. Read them'

LOUISE WELSH

'These essential poems perfectly capture the "dreadful shipwreck" of not being easily categorised as one thing or another in a world that already resists writing you into its histories. Hannah's words reveal the enormous strength required to heal that fracture'

MARJORIE LOTFI

'Lavery's poems lift the woman from the margins. Often dark, sometimes hilarious, occasionally brutal, *Unwritten Woman* is a vital look at our culture through the lens of the other'

JIM MONAGHAN

ABOUT THE AUTHOR

Hannah Lavery is a poet and playwright from Edinburgh, named by Owen Sheers as one of the Ten Writers Asking Questions That Will Shape Our Future. Her debut poetry collection *Blood Salt Spring* (Polygon) was nominated for a Saltire Prize in 2022 and named as one of the Poetry Society Books of the Year. Hannah is the current Makar (poet laureate) for the City of Edinburgh, and a former associate artist with the National Theatre of Scotland.

UNWRITTEN WOMAN

Hannah Lavery

Polygon

First published in paperback in Great Britain in 2024 by Polygon,
an imprint of Birlinn Ltd | West Newington House | 10 Newington Road
Edinburgh | EH9 1QS

9 8 7 6 5 4 3 2 1

www.polygonbooks.co.uk

Copyright © Hannah Lavery, 2024

The right of Hannah Lavery to be identified as the author of this work has been asserted in accordance with the Copyright, Designs and Patents Act 1988.

All rights reserved. No part of this publication may be reproduced, stored, or transmitted in any form, or by any means electronic, mechanical or photocopying, recording or otherwise, without the express written permission of the publisher.

ISBN 978 1 84697 665 0
eBook ISBN 978 1 78885 676 8

British Library Cataloguing-in-Publication Data
A catalogue record for this book is available from the British Library.

The publisher acknowledges support from the National Lottery through Creative Scotland towards the publication of this title.

Typeset in Adobe Caslon Pro by The Foundry, Edinburgh
Printed and bound in Great Britain by Clays Ltd, Elcograf S.p.A.

*For Adrian and our children,
and in memory of my father.*

CONTENTS

edinburgh (is a story)   xv

Author's Note   xix

PART ONE:
The Strange Case of ~~Dr Jekyll and Mr Hyde~~
the Unwritten Women   1

PART TWO:
Unwritten (...)   75

Acknowledgements   135
With Love and Thanks   136

Sràid nam Marbh

i'm always (was always) will always be

the girl who threw herself
down like a challenge
to the world / this mornin
i haled her to her feet / as i walked
this street of the dead / left her standin
by st columba / to join my sisters
dancin at the shore.

edinburgh (is a story)

My father another walking ghost finding this city as it was and can never be again.

Memory is a shifting thing, like this city it cannot be relied upon.

Like Hutton discovered in the rock we are layers upon layers; lives built upon lives. If you reach out you can feel our dead. We don't let them lie here in their shallow graves. We dig them up. Offer them eternity in drunken tales.

They live on in the haar. They will run you down. Come at you as sharp as the rain comes. As unrelenting.

My father said he dreamt of these streets in his sleep but like his dreams these streets flit. If you spend too long away you will find they have changed just enough to remind you that time has passed. Hutton in Salisbury Crags. Time showing itself.

A deep abyss. It can be a dangerous place if you want to hold on to your certainty.

I can't be sure but looking back at ourselves there is nothing here that offers that sort of comfort.

It is a hard place for faith. The imagination threatens you like the weather here.

We hold no truck with neat endings. It is a never-ending still-to-be-done place; cradled by seven hills (made in fire, made in water) and we struggle still with the spark and the urge to dampen it.

We mock surety in the flyting. We will make you cry and then we will carry you up to see the world as it is . . .

Our good doctors turning devil in the middle passage; our daft wee gadges, satirical poets rich wi contradiction; our dinnie get above yoursel, wind ye neck ins; our communities of wash yer step tenement dwellers; our appointed: worthy folk, midwives of the imperial dream. Our better nature caught wi his flies doun (passing around the plate . . .)

Our pious preachers greedy for mission, mad cunts and fuck you ravers; our students sizing up heads. Radical teachers dreaming in soft beds *once upon a* . . .

Our brass neck revolutionaries growing organised: in city slum, in committee room. Our bankers playing gods, cruising Mount Olympus, comin doun, aw broken promise. Our great men twisting the knot on enlightened thinking tae forever justify bloody dominion. We see you . . .

Well-pissed weighing up our good against our fucking awful. . . The Father who loves you (like the moon reflects light).

For all our Dr Jekylls, our Mr Hydes. Our history: the not so dormant volcano, throwing out rock. Making new hit. New pit. New vista (again and again).

Don't think this is telt yet. Our story is not a fixed thing. Don't come here for anything as limiting as clarity, as reductive as forward momentum. Our tale has a sting. It bites.

You will hurt if you try to lay us out. There is always a close you did not account for (the snakes and the ladders). Our steep hills will lead you down more often than up.

It is a brave soul (a rare soul even) that looks up to the sky.

But if vision is found there be sure we will claim it as if it were our own. They said once that you could not stand a moment in this city without touching genius. We smile at that as if it was true of us all (as if it was true of any of us). Our genius is a contested thing. Good luck to you . . .

Good luck if you want to claim it as pure light. Be careful of that, there are traps built in . . .

But at the shore (droukit wi the greetin) you will find him. Lookin out at aw that working sea . . . My father.

[The haar rolls back in]

'If I didn't define myself for myself, I would be crunched into other people's fantasies for me and eaten alive'

AUDRE LORDE

AUTHOR'S NOTE

What follows are poems imagining and reimagining the women at the edges of Robert Louis Stevenson's *The Strange case of Dr Jekyll and Mr Hyde*, with extracts from the novel acting as titles to the poems. Lines from the poems then become titles to further poems in response.

PART ONE

THE STRANGE CASE OF
~~DR JEKYLL AND MR HYDE~~ THE
UNWRITTEN WOMEN

The Strange Case of Dr Jekyll and Mr Hyde the Unwritten Women

its spine runs us through. he tells me
it's *the truth of this city*. i see her
in the margins. wonder
what she knew.

DRAMATIS PERSONAE

~~enfield~~
~~utterson~~
~~poole~~
~~dr jekyll / mr hyde~~
witness / the poet
agnes / the cook
annie / the insurgent
girl / the wounded
maid / the soldier
mother / the fallen
sarah / the dreamer
conscience / who waits
the madwomen / who have
always known

the rising panic. say *hello to your buried phantom.* ready yourself to take the bitter pill. *steady* yourself until the alarm & next door's early start signals you survived it all. the rising panic. say *hello to your buried phantom.* ready yourself to take the bitter pill. *steady* yourself until the alarm & next door's early start signals you survived it all. the rising panic. say *hello to your buried phantom* ready yourself to take the bitter pill. say *hello to your buried phantom.* ready yourself to take the bitter pill. *steady* yourself until the alarm & next door's early start signals you survived it all ... his rising panic. dance with *your buried phantom.* show early signals you survived it. all your rising panic. say *come in to your buried phantom.* give yourself the bitter pill. *steady rock steady* **insomnia** & next door's early start signals you survived your rising panic. say *hello to your buried father.* ready yourself to take the bitter pill. *steal* yourself until the alarm & next door's early start signals you'll survive it all. say *hello to your buried girl.* ready yourself to be the bitter pill. *steady* yourself until the alarm says steady yourself & next door's scream signals the rising panic. *hello to your buried* self. take bitter pill. until the alarm. *steady. steady* yourself until the alarm & next door's early start signals you survived it all. the rising panic. say *hello to your buried phantom.* ready yourself to take the bitter pill. *steady* yourself until the alarm ... *steady* yourself until next door's digging signals you won't survive. the rising panic. say *fuck it. fuck it. phantom* **says** *hello.* take the bitter pill ... *ready steady* ... the alarm. early start signals the rising panic ... say steady yourself. take the bitter pill. the next signal is the rising panic ... say *hello to your buried phantom* ... ready yourself to take bitter pill ... *steady* your hand ... rid yourself ... until the alarm & next door signals ... you survived it aw ... the rising panic ... say *hello to your buried phantom* ... ready yourself to take bitter pill ... *steady* ... *steady* yourself ... until the alarm & next door ... **hi** ... signals you'll survive the rising panic ... steady ... be the bitter pill say *hello* ... *say hello* ... the rising panic. say *hello to your buried phantom.* ready yourself to take the bitter pill. *steady* yourself. until the alarm & next door's early start signals you survived it all. the rising panic. say *hello to your buried phantom.* ready yourself to take the bitter pill. *steady* yourself. until the alarm & next door's early start signals you survived it all. the rising panic. say *hello to your buried phantom.* ready yourself to take the bitter pill. say *hello to your buried phantom.* ready yourself to take the bitter pill. *steady* yourself until the alarm & next door's early start signals you survived it all. the rising panic. say *hello to your buried phantom.* ready yourself to take the bitter pill. dance with *your buried girl.* say *come in.* say *hello to your buried phantom.* ready yourself. steady their rising. be the bitter pill ... say *hello* ... *say hello* ... *say hello* ...

'. . . and through the muffle and smother of these fallen clouds, the procession of the town's life was still rolling in . . .'

poem of the passing,
of the way he stood

in the street. the night
taking him in.

spilt lip

on the turn. spoons of sugar
laid waste; the uneaten tray.

warring welt

springing fae scurrying rats, searching
fur new ship, settling fur drowning.

torn slip

piling the fire wi more wood, never able
tae throw the shakes; the cold creep,

creeping
up the backstairs.

oh, my son.
what are you?

counting the pile in the carpet. noting
the quality of veneer. straining

tae see
the mountains.

mercy. too distant. a memory.
to ask for. prostrate on the pavement.

in rage. frae amongst the dust. in skin
shed. in blood. the squall

hauls heavy . . .
frae the rot, frae the truth;

under the perfume,
the women.

under the perfume
(part one)

1.
i explained death
to my daughter

(. . . sharing the laptop)

watched our deaths
move toward us

(. . . like haar).

2.
she stands

for another year
in a chamber of echoes

prepares to list our
dead –

they cut to an old man
in his of hall of mirrors

(before she has even
finished saying our . . .).

3.
still meet you
on our battered bench
in the square

still drink our good
rum in bone-cold
embrace

still while ye tell me
in the whip of it all
that you're done

      wi jist coping . . .

still when the dead
night draws in . . .

still. still. still
find myself

reachin
(. . . for you).

'. . . the man trampled calmly over the child's body and left her screaming on the ground. It sounds nothing to hear, but it was hellish to see.'

running from a broken mother.
jigsaw girl. abacus girl. to be added up

and counted. costed for market day.
crushed under boot. stunned silent

to shrieking like a freedom
on hard stone street.

nine going on ten
but i'm too old already,

i feel ma days: spent
pricks, cold coins

stacked. the hoard
at ma back.

he comes & i'm sent
frae her bed. he comes

& she sends me oot
tae sleep in the hall,

tae count the minutes
on ma fingers & toes.

[counts on her fingers]

she calls
for a doctor

as he runs
down the stairs.

i wait

[counts on her fingers]

then go
howl at my feet.

enfield
haund tae the wall

tae steady
his world ...

girl distracted
by his transformation

from fury
in her mother's bed

to pitiful wretch
in his father's suit.

& aw of this (if you
can imagine) is playing

oot in my head / already so laden / aw of this
is playing oot / rewinding back / forwarding fast tae my mother
pleading fur the doctor / when i'm met by a wall at the corner
where a corner shoulda been

only hard stone man.

[whispers of hyde]

& this new demon
moves like a wave

of every hurt (left
by every bolting man)

& frae here
i can see the stars.

i've never seen stars
so beautiful, so bright,

so many. a chapel. a chorus
glistening back tae me,

rare welcome
(come fur me)

i'd count them,
but I'm no sure

where i left
ma fingers & toes.

i'm no sure
where i left ma body

was it here?

did i have it
when i left her?

[the light dims]

playing oot in my head

filled wi rough takings,
screaming (harpy in a cage).

leaving you (my darling girl)
knees bruised and bleeding.

'. . . killing being out of the question, we did the next best.'

[conscience steps forward]

& enfield joins them
in the harsh light

(of good men)

he joins them ashen
from across the street

& i come
like a whisper

as he shakes her blood
from his wringing hands.

i am the girl
counting

the minutes on her
fingers & toes

the stars spinning (with all
her numbered days).

her numbered days

my bag sat like a memory of a child (by the door that
failed to slam ...)

you came home to tell me that you had
never loved me; told me like i should already know,
but i really believed it was love.

three months later i left. leaving only red wine stains
(and the memory of blood).

that dent in the wall you made with your fist, i
patched up. the ash of my poems you encouraged
me to burn, i scattered on next door's rose (i let so much go).

i forget the address now (it has been such a long time)
but i remember the shape of it. that you had gone by
the time i finally did. that i took my time locking up.

that i sat in the empty room with the
memory of our bed; an echo on the carpet:
your delight when you danced naked to marvin gaye,
wiggling your snake hips, your proud cock pulsing to
the bass line ...

i stayed on the floor until i was dimmed to a quiet
light. dull keen. until i was dead leg. fading faint. blue
bruise ... then i left (left you dancin with dust motes).

i took my bag; i walked away.

'. . . as we were pitching it in red hot, we were keeping the
women off him as best we could, for they were as wild as
harpies . . .'

[the witness at her window]

they say i am only sleight
of hand; a faint pulse

beating (& it beats when i see
him there. is he unwell?) aye but,

there is something there
that warns me / reminds me

of the stories my grandmother
used to tell. i turn down my light

& remain watching. as he moves.
as she falls. i get ready to go

to her but there is a round of men
with their blood up. tongues

out. tails wagging. still. still her screaming
brings her women. her mother walks

painfully (a corpse
already) to her wailing child

& i think of the madonna. fanciful
notions. Good & Evil.

for it is Evil the men think
they see in him

but in truth
it is only themselves

(their relief is palpable)

the man is come
who will take away their sin.

her screaming
the sideshow

this devil
the thing

(shadow man)

the honourable
enfield walks away

(scot-free)

the dying girl
lies on the street

with her dying
mother. forgotten.

they go with him,
these men

(prowling the night)

they go with him
for his hush money

(& absolution).

they seek
their redemption.

go straight
to the back door

of doctor jekyll
with their hands out

(for their hand out).

i watch them.
i write it all down

& he turns

this good man's
familiar,

looks up to me
at my window.

warns me / reminds me

                                  when my body was my very own,
                             when i could feel the strength of it;
                               delight in it when catching it move
                                  in the tall mirrors of dance class.

left my body when i was
only just grown. have never

fully returned to it. only
visited it in moments.

was told that the past
stays there but it comes back

at three a.m.
i sit in the dark with it.

the open wound
staining our bed.

think about
the cold anaesthesia

rushing through my body,
as i count backwards,

an incantation:
a spell of surrender.

how often have i played
that prayer on my lips?

to escape your own body;

let the cold fill your veins
(wake without memory).

'. . . into the great kitchen, where the fire was out and the beetles were leaping on the floor.'

[agnes alone]

i hear the whispers
capture them like sugar water

falling leaves caught
in gutters

dr jekyll?

she works head down
breath held in his kitchen.

his name creaking
floorboards in the night,

mr hyde?

a cold that comes in
from hidden clefts.

his voice, a cat shut out
in the cold, my ears bleed

with it. he steps closer out
of the dank of the landing.

i move back,
flat back

against the wall.
& still he comes . . .

i'm a small bird,
a linnet.

i am hungry, he says.
a small linnet. a finch.

the sweet song. feeding them
scraps of girl in the yard.

watching them from the
wee window in the pantry,

those unshowy birds.
my father would have

trapped one,
put it in a cage

for the priest.
i am trying

to recall their song.
those fluttering hearts.

their sweet wee voices.
my father would have

caged them.
brought them indoors

for the parlour,
for the sunday visits.

i preferred them in the yard.
fleeting wee things

you're not yourself.

later i hear her
from my bed

but i'm not for
climbing those stairs

to her (not now
i'm bird seed).

my father would have caged them

she dances in the sea,
old promise pinned
to her neoprene,

barnacles, fragile clasp
to her second skin,
grow thin to words

on paper, they will make her
concertina: a hundred more
pleats in her creases;

seaweed & shell pulled
from her nail beds; her lost
things: conch shell & mixtape

greet her like lovers
at the break which she
teeters towards on tiptoes

of glass; cracking,
breaking open
in each step;

her hard hips
holding ...
old desire.

as she threatens
to soar, to dip, to take
flight with the gannets,

to learn the secrets
of their horizon. a man,
an apparition appears

(as he always appears)

like he has just risen
from the dunes, a mass
of sharp grass, sinking slope;

spit up of sandflies.
a bloody disgrace
he proclaims

from his dog shit
pulpit. his odious
overflow: remembered

slap. she stops stone,
an icicle in a two-step.
gathered up.

packed away in
stripped shopper.
leaving

her dance
in the sand (like
contrails in the air).

'. . . until the clock of the neighbouring church rang out the hour of twelve, when he would go soberly and gratefully to bed.'

   in his study we are equals. while it is dark; while the lamps are needed.
   he would say he wants me only for his bed but that is not the truth (& if he was quiet enough he would know it).
   i offer him my silence & his whisky
& in the depths of his night . . .
   he moans & calls out *jekyll*.

depths of his night
(the housecat)

they agree she will play stupid,
when he comes home humiliated,

they agree somewhere before the
face-down fucking, shortly after

her advice, that it will be better
if she took to her knees. silent

(but for her mocking purr).

'It was his custom of a Sunday, when his meal was over, to sit close by the fire, a volume of some dry divinity on his reading desk'

[annie sits with her mr utterson]

but he seems incapable of saying anything
more. so we sit a while longer the night
laid out in front of us . . .

[taking out her notebook]

matching his high, making sure
to bring shock into my voice . . .

[noting him down]

catching my reflection in his tipped glass,
bringing my hand to my open mouth . . .

[putting down her pen]

shall i seek him out?

[closing her book]

taking more of his whisky.

[settling herself into his good chair]

taking more of his whisky

        (i match yer whisky drinkin)

    catchin emmers   aw languid lilt
an saftly furl   rollin tae the edge   dancin
dancin it ower   tae lettin it   aw the hinnie
linger ... (i'll be takin yer hale nicht ...)
        tae finish.

'. . . O my poor old Henry Jekyll, if ever I read Satan's signature upon a face, it is on that of your new friend.'

she knows the devil
as much as she is known

by him. stalks him. takes her place
amongst the mad & the forgotten,

who gather watching for him,
in all his finery & demon clothes.

at the good doctor's door,
she sees how

he means to
change himself.

knows a man
who has abandoned me.

she who carries me
with her like a mother

(she who will
tear it all down).

she knows the devil
(the lichen, the devil & me)

      i was transfixed
      by you,

    a mathematical beauty,

     form
     like a dream i had
     (or a test i always failed)

            i was talking to him

     but focussed
     on my fingers
     running over the ridges

of your skin

     following you
     like a labyrinth
     to some edge of a knowing,

     i talked on

     while remembering
     that you are a sign
     of good air

          & in his eyes
          he tried to hold me
            steady.

    & i wondered

about the nature
of clarity

        & he held a silence
        like the opening bars
        of a song

& untethered
i tried

to take in
the rarity of a breath

        but he told me a story
        which held a question
        about life

& with my fingers
resting

on the sharp cliff
of you

i wanted

to trace you   on his skin,

in all your intricacy,

a navigational chart,
to a home

i once knew.

'. . . at night under the face of the fogged city moon, by all lights and at all hours of solitude or concourse, ~~the lawyer~~ was to be found on ~~his~~ chosen post.'

for three nights annie watches sarah's house:

the good men come when their good clubs
close. when their gavel is laid down. when the
policemen light their way – clearing their
paths – their gold falling like good manners.

for three nights she watches him:

on the fourth day she strips herself, layer by layer. slice by slice. wraps herself up like a patient. in her beggar shawls walks (straight by her utterson as he leaves him again at dawn).

clearing their paths

i know how to
walk this city at night,

to move with a pace learnt
when keeping up with my mother.

rushing to the arc of streetlamps,
holding myself fawn-like

in the sweep of headlights
passing over,

listening (head on
straight tight neck)

for a scream left
in my bathroom,

fixed under
foundation.

[let nothing out]

keeping my face
etching on stone

carve in a smile.

look down before
it's read as invitation.

[invite nothing]

remember my grandmother's
teaching: *walk in the middle*

of the street, not too close
to the stair. not too close

to the curb. join her seance
for the missing girls; let

the creeping haar come.
go missing.

[become nothing]

with a look of his daughter, with a look
of his mother, with a look of his teacher.

[teach him nothing]

sit at the front of the night bus, sit
with the women on the last train home.

when the men come take note
of which of you is most vulnerable.

catch her eye.

[do nothing. say nothing.
feel nothing . . . be nothing].

'. . . many women of many different nationalities passing out, key in hand, to have a morning glass; and the next moment the fog settled down again . . .'

an ye think
we drink tae forget

but we drink tae brave you,

walking amongst us
like watchman; we steal

yer key tae free oorselves,
tae dance like wild hings:

drunken moths mad birlin
in diffused light.

drunken moths

we make a throne
out of our empties

sit like kings,
holding on

to the last
of each other;

we watch
the sun rise

between us,
our feet soaking

in the swill,
our hearts

breakin again
in the leavin.

'She had an evil face, smoothed by hypocrisy; but her manners were excellent.'

mr hyde?

took to his rooms
some two months back.

[sarah smiles]

i see you in those shawls, annie,
you're safe now. come now,

share a pot of tea with me.

[annie takes off her shawls]

he is a grand one, that's for sure,
turkish carpets lain across the floor,

have the burns on me still.

[they take a moment to drink their tea]

but annie,
he's not like them others.

i hear him weeping. fretful
dreams he has. terrible dreams,

you'd almost feel something for him

[annie reaches for her hand]

but there is the devil there,
make no mistake.

you know it, when a man plays
out his storms on you.

[annie adds sugar to her cup]

he has this painting on his wall,
i look upon it when he –

[annie nods]

but it's such a thing, annie,
to find beauty here. mountains,

and a clear spring that wends its way
down the valley. this green valley

& nestled in this brick cottage,
a wisp of smoke rising from its chimney.

i could fancy myself living there,
and under a sky of blue,

such clear skies, i have been very taken
with that, annie.

it has been a long while since
i saw the mountains,

and i mean to go back
when i grow too old

for this, i will go back,
drink from that stream.

[she pours annie another cup]

and then i would finally fall
under all that perfect blue.

[they drink their tea in silence]

if you mean to do him harm,
you will get no noise from me

[they put down their teacups]

but would you leave me
the painting, annie?

plays out his storms

we hold our faces
in the deep blue bruising;

like the ball we failed to catch,
like the rare bird that flew away

too quickly. we hold the
fleeting to our faces,

like glimpses of something
we failed to see.

'You sit quietly on the top of a hill; and away the stone goes, starting others; and presently some bland old bird (the last you would have thought of) is knocked on the head in ~~his~~ own back garden . . .'

[conscience enters]

conscience, he calls,
like to a mother. like a lover

i come. i have been circling his dreams.
pouring myself into his slack jaw,

cured of the devil! he cries
and i watch hyde go,

his tail ripped clean off
by the swing of the door;

the good doctor settles
himself by my side.

i am his conscience;
he whispers, *i am returned.*

i am the cook in her kitchen
feeding her precious birds.

i am the maid finding her
legs like a new foal.

he has returned.
i return

he announces, inviting
the good men again to dine.

the good men again to dine

in the morning she sweeps out
the ashes with her sisters,
they bring them in

shaking shovels
(still smoking) to the pile
at the end of the garden.

set it down
by the other, full
with the peelings.

today their father will
cook the bird for the
sunday roast

& they will sit
nicely, pretending
they haven't

spent their day
clearing out
yesterday's fire.

"'Utterson, I swear to God," cried the doctor, "I swear to God I will never set eyes on him again. I bind my honour to you that I am done with him in this world.'"

[annie puts her knife back]

just when i think
i have the devil caught

utterson returns

to his glum parlour sitting,
weak urges and i'm left

[whispers of jekyll]

stealing his whisky,
playing his part –

[whispers of hyde]

glum parlour sitting

i've been drawing your body in my mind,
holding you like a combed shell to my ear:

to my own name said like prayer.

meeting you again in a crowd (shamed
by my own imagination) i put you back

on the shore,

watch for the turn of the tide; wait for the sea
to return (to wash my secret from you).

'Now that evil influence had been withdrawn, a new life began for Dr Jekyll.'

& in his house, his women
are sweeping out past days.

she has rearranged herself (saucer
to cup) to hide the bruises.

the kitchen hums.

the linnets are come
to the yard.

what can i tell you?

he returned to us.
he came downstairs

restored. i said, mr hyde?
and he looked at me

for a long moment. hyde?
hyde is gone, he said

and i had to stop myself
from falling at his feet.

[the linnets sing]

they are not much
to look at, are they?

but their song, it's beautiful,
don't you think?

agnes, you are hurt.
it's nothing.

but agnes?
he is gone.

it seems that way, i say.
their laughter coming down

to us. she offers me tea.
we sit by the fire

& in her kitchen
you could for a moment

believe that all was right
in the world,

but if you look hard
you can see the cup

in her hand tremble.
if you look hard

enough, you can see
the whole house shakes.

the whole house shakes

he watches her dancin
wi her sisters

wraps her in a cloud
(blinding her to

the shore) a cloud
like wire wool . . .

she becomes mother
to snow. his stay-at-home

deity; falling
sugar drops

into neon
plastic tumblers;

cave dweller
watching light

falling on walls.
they've created

marks on her
(like tree rings)

& she longs to run,
stretch out like a summer,

bound barefoot
beyond the trellis;

the fallen climber; praying
his thunder will strike

her clear back
to the sea.

open as the mouth
at her breast, as the

possibility of change
in the weather.

'A fortnight later, by excellent good fortune, the doctor gave one of his pleasant dinners to some five or six old cronies, all intelligent, reputable men and all judges of good wine; and Mr Utterson so contrived that he remained behind after the others had departed.'

[annie stands alone]

he returns to Jekyll. the soldier passes by carrying their dirty plates (the rats following her) and i take a glass left by one of those grand loud men (wipe it on the hem of my dress) put it up to the closed door.

Grand Loud Men
(what you see is what you get)

she shows him her broken things:

a doll without a head, a torn painting
of the night.

there is no art here,
he says.

pushing her out
(into the cold).

'The rosy man had grown pale; his flesh had fallen away; he was visibly balder and older; and yet it was not so much these tokens of a swift physical decay that arrested the ~~lawyer's~~ notice, as a look in the eye . . .'

i watch him as he makes a show
of his new-found goodness,

his return is a gold road.
a glistening path to her door

where his childhood
things still hang.

mother!
he calls

& then
he started to speak

of the madwomen.
begged me for their spells,

i have none i said
& he looked at me

with this –
(how can i tell you?)

i saw him leave.
on his little red bike.

he left me
&

he left him
here with me.

this is not my son!
this is not my son!

can you not hear her?

this is not my son!

a glistening path
(safety advice)

we teach you your first word
marvel at your first step,

we watch you grow
into boys / into men;

worry that you will forget
how you held our hands

as we led you into the world
& we long to pull you back

safe like the way we taught
you to carry scissors:

the blade out / towards us.

'It seems she was romantically given, for she sat down upon her box, which stood immediately under the window, and fell into a dream of musing.'

a woman should not be a poet.
witness in her garret *is a fanciful one*

they'll whisper. the coroner's report
will misspell her name, but she cares nothing

for their spells (she has spells of her own)
in her high window, dancin wi the heavens

i see ye,
good doctor. standing there

for yer medicine. but they'll offer
ye nae more silence

she'll nae be forgotten.

i'll summon vengeance
fae here wi ma pen

call doon the angels
tae sharp point.

a woman should not be a poet.

(but i feel so much safer when i leave
my body at the door to my room)

'You must suffer me to go my own dark way.'

[they speak out from the edges. they come in
from the shadows (from out of the cold . . .)]

the 'good'
come to us.

a penny?
(a penny of your fortune).

we cast a spell
to offer them a freedom.

run along . . .
but still they come,

thinking that they can –
oh?

that is not how this works.
smiling we grind our spices

to ease the separation.
we take her in

& feed her oranges

but still they come
(for her . . .)

my darlin,
my darlin,

cast me
yer lion.

turn me
tae steel.

make me
yer armour,

build me
tae barricade

           (. . . i'll take their blows)

count me
a kindness

label me
trying . . .

leave me
tae witness

           (. . . i know who you are)

bury me
deep / root.

plant me
tae meadow.

break me . . .

                                        (. . . would they break us all?)

into the new day . . .

my darlin,
my darlin,

                                        (. . . i'll take their blows).

"'Now, my good man," ~~said the lawyer,~~ "be explicit. What are you afraid of?'"

[annie stands]

the door knocks.
utterson lies

like a child
wrapped around me.

the door knocks.
he is not himself, i say.

none of them are,
poole whispers,

none of them ever are.

[poole exits]

child wrapped around me

i lie all night bereft
of my own peace; keep myself
down to a whisper (. . . you sleep on).

none of them ever are

over drinks you pinned
me down with your

attention. later i think
it was such good luck

to find myself
(. . . discarded on your floor).

'I have been doomed to such a dreadful shipwreck: that man is not truly one, but truly two. I say two, because the state of my own knowledge does not pass beyond that point.'

& when we arrive
at his trembling house

the rats are gathering
at the gates,

they look at me with pity (i think
i hear them pray for me).

i think i hear them pray for me

long hidden in grass
and nettle. this ribbon
from my hair will mark her

our unwritten woman
to the low branch
of the yew,

yellow ribbon,
a pigeon's feather;
pilgrimage

and when the rain comes
(like it often does) from under the overhang
of the church roof

i will watch
sloping gravel paths
between the dead overflow

into capillary,
into a rash of burns
running over

'. . . the housemaid broke into hysterical whimpering . . .'

agnes &
the rest of the house

are gathered in the hall.
the men have decided

but she **sees**
my intention

& calls on all
our terror.

our terror

she told you she was uncomfortable,

& you told her *he's like that with everyone
lighten up / it's just the drink /* listed his good deeds / played
out his wounds / counted all that you owed: told her she was
mistaken.

>she flew her damned flight,
>into a mountain of men.

if only she had said something

>her words in plain sight.

'Right in the midst there lay the body of a man sorely
contorted and still twitching. They drew near on tiptoe,
turned it on its back and beheld the face of Edward Hyde.
He was dressed in clothes far too large for him, clothes of
the doctor's bigness . . .'

his dead mother holds open his locked door
for me. i walk in & feel others walk in too.

scores of us.

their whispers create a draft. the curtains
blow by closed windows & there he is

standing before us
shaking.

conscience sits by the fire. she has
made the tea, offers me china cup,

he has wet himself. rocks like a
cradle on his heels.

his mother shakes her head.
sarah paints the mountains.

the madwomen write *fuck off*
in the margins of the good book,

& a little girl dances
with her mother in the starlight.

& all the while he stands there.
pissing & weeping. dr jekyll / mr hyde.

fixed like a saint to his stake,
while we dance & sing our songs,

summon more of our sisters,
as we drink our tea & load up the fire,

jekyll's mother whispers her words to
her beautiful boy dying in her arms

& just before they all make it in –

      we are gone.

  the kettle bubbles over. a china cup lies ready. the good
  book lies open, scrawled with our blasphemy. and a
  small boy lies dead, drowned in a good man's clothes.

insomnia

Drinking tea in silence. Watching the snow fall.
Sometimes this waking brings such beauty. Rare
moment. Rare for its insistence.

'Some women get erased a little at a time, some all at once. Some reappear. Every woman who appears wrestles with the forces that would have her disappear. She struggles with the forces that would tell her story for her, or write her out of the story, the genealogy, the rights of man, the rule of law. The ability to tell your own story, in words or images, is already a victory, already a revolt.'

REBECCA SOLNIT

under the perfume
(part two)

the Trojan women
wait at the brink

of their burning city.

Cassandra silently
mouths the future

at the edge
of the shore

her tears fall,
silently salting

the sea:

no one listened to me.

no one believed me.

(i'll believe you).

PART TWO

UNWRITTEN (. . .)

[sounds of the shore]

silt: sharp seeps

salt: shore the scars

[sound of swimming]

seaweed strays

slow (down) sure sea

sings (back to me)

[sounds of the surf]

was always

(will always)

has always –

[the sea]

Dad?

Daddy's Gone

wasn't i the one you left to grow up
in the shadow of Easter Road to be
your Edinburgh girl carrying on
your words treasure
(fur ye to find)

DRAMATIS PERSONAE

poet / swims
her daddy / goes
his daughter / remains
her brown girl / birlin
her nana / by the clock
shasta / her light
clementine / her beauty
jackie kay / her pole star
young fathers / her pacemaker
alberta whittle / her break in the haar
her son / her everything
four poets of colour / at *abolition corner*
john agard / reverberation
loyle carner / reverberating
the specials / their saturday school
edwin morgan / with the starlings
john maclean / murmuration
rev dr george turner / bird catcher
rabid dog / the wounded; wounding
golliwog / at the *Museum of Childhood*
theatre announcer / pronounces (from on high)

THEATRE ANNOUNCEMENT

Ladies & gentlemen please take your seats
for tonight's performance of *Falling off a Cliff*

(of her own making).

Jackie tells us about the time Audre Lorde told her she could be Black and Scottish – elongating the *and*. I say that *and* is the thing. Aye it is. Aye it is, is maybe what she says back to me

aye Scottish an intae the sea
(fur the dook) cursing

aw that bloody cauld
tae running raucous

ruby raw (a bunch o loons)
aw tangled an tinselled (wi regret).

aye, knowing aw the words,
an whit is really being said. aye

but still singing. aye still haudin back
yer tongue. wind yer neck in an

leave it, pal. know where
ye belong an who ye

belong tae. fuck me
that view. aye that

(bloody view). auld traces.
paper (towns) aye?

THEATRE ANNOUNCEMENT

[holding open the door]

Look I understand
the need for diversity,
he winks, but what
about quality, eh?

Person of Colour

coloured in half-caste strokes
paki(ed) in neat box, high
(on) yellow(ing) shelf. oot
of the dark(ie). doggy
in the windae, ~~wag~~ wog ing
its ~~tail~~ tale. belly up!

THEATRE ANNOUNCEMENT

Please get your refund at the box office.
The show is over. The cost was too high.

Coloured Girl Goes to a Party
After Ntozake Shange

at a house party
i take out my cassette.

purple rain all ready
cued up to play.

i turn up the volume.
step back.

wait.

                              purple rain,
                              purple rain, purple –

& he is the only one
that gets it

& he doesn't let me
dance alone. we leap

over empty bottles
& beer cans to each other.

stepping over stoned
boys. laughing

as we do our best
impressions. air guitar,

thrusting hips. heads
thrown back,

take a breather
in the backyard. sigh

when Oasis goes back
on & i go on and on

about my love
of Prince.

all the while.
ignoring . . .

>*only want*
>*to see you dancing*

(some part of me
is being stolen)

he is . . .
on his knees

in the damp yard looking
for where he has dropped

his lighter. finds it. lights
a cigarette. looking at me,

the edge of me lit by him
in the dark. he calls me

his ms kama sutra. *23 positions*

in a one-night stand

(except there is only ever
really one). he sings

                                                         purple rain

lets his hands
roam me once more . . .

only stopping to take another
drag on his cigarette.

winking at me (zipping himself up)
he leaves. hands me the dog end

of his rollie (he takes my body
with him). he leaves me

this body (so much
like my own).

THEATRE ANNOUNCEMENT

We apologise, tonight's show is cancelled.
Please feel free to do your own show.
We have left the lights on.

o my brown girl

counting the ceiling
tiles. laid oot

on a scummy sheet. hiding
in a stranger's bathroom,

matching yoursel
tae the moths that birl

in through windaes (too wee
tae climb through).

THEATRE ANNOUNCEMENT

You are all very drunk. Slurring your words & missing your marks. The theatre bar is no place for pretending you are sincere (or that you liked their play).

She tells me she knows how to get rid of those streaks of egg from our windows. God, they always got the window facing the bus stop, I say. Waiting for the school bus, avoiding the stares of dried yolk on the glass. We laugh about that (all these years later).

the eggs of monarch butterflies grow
rare in patches of milkweed found
at the edges of all their perfect lawns.

Coloured Girl Went to a Party
After Ntozake Shange

sitting in the gloaming
behind the beach wall.

fingernails
dirty wi tobacco.

knees still bruised
like a girl's knees,

like i climb trees,
like i'm all kind of free.

my body is tender shoot
under heavy fleece

and i think it will break
before it blooms . . .

they've been coming
in the afternoons

like stray dogs in heat.
letting themselves in

by the back gate. bringing
cheap cider to grease

the lock. circling
like a pack . . .

sitting in the gloaming
behind the beach wall.

fingernails
dirty wi tobacco.

cunt like broken glass,
like a midge bite . . .

they have been throwing
eggs at my window.

they've been leaving
me notes, scrawled

with protractors
on their desks,

with their shit,
on toilet doors.

waiting like vultures
for skin, tit, thigh,

behind the bike sheds.
down by the burn.

& i burn. set a fire.
come to them

like a blaze.
leave them ashes

(throw back their
cum like mercy)

sitting in the gloaming
behind the beach wall

fingernails
dirty wi tobacco

the haar calling
me in

salt air
curing. the sea

brings its shells
& i crush them to white

powder. wear it
like a war cry.

THEATRE ANNOUNCEMENT

We would like to apologise
for the playwright of colour
having a breakdown in the foyer.

We would like you to know
we are aware of the problem.

I find myself saying when questioned, in an attempt to cement something, that my father was a black man. But maybe he was a brown man or was he only ever half a man . . .

half mythic?

(i find myself after all
these dead years

still looking for him
that familiar rush

threatening to topple
me anxious again

that the gap between
step and platform

will widen and
take him away

i become
an obstacle

on the busy
thoroughfare

listening
for a ghost . . .)

darling,
i'm over here.

THEATRE ANNOUNCEMENT

We are excited to announce that we have added an extra performance of *White People Erasure*. A satirical look at all things woke by the good white playwright.

Starlings (in the Square)

> 'I wonder if we really deserve starlings?'
> Edwin Morgan

who are the starlings?

are we the starlings, Edwin?

(to be understood only as their metaphor. seen only in
their reflection. poor relation. appreciated but as
disruption. much needed jolt. tolerated like medicine.
the sunday lesson. the temporary upset. the latest fad?)

who are the poets, Edwin?

are we the starlings?

(come only to disturb their world).

THEATRE ANNOUNCEMENT

We would like to apologise
for the playwrights of colour
having breakdowns in the foyer.

We would like you to know
we are very aware of the problem.

On seeing Alberta Whittle's exhibition,
Create Dangerously, with my friend at the
Scottish gallery of modern art in Edinburgh

she stands fixed to a spot
in front of a series of self portraits
of Alberta Whittle

in the modern art gallery
in Edinburgh. *her body is like my body*
she says. *all her beauty is like my own*

like she is whispering to some secret
part of herself. *beautiful*. she turns
back to me. sitting on

a parenthesis.

we walk round the rest
of the exhibition as if holding hands.
in the sunshine we complain

about the cost of our salads,
and i think to tell her what she means
to me but instead take her empty plate

back to the counter; wiping
the crumbs from our table
(with my sleeve).

i can never come back to you,

but i try to hear your voice. the way you said, *darling*.
   i can always hear her. call her up as easy as deep breath but for you i'm trying ...
   your voice. the one i was so many more times without. that came without touch through the telephone. listening.
looping cord tightly, cat's cradle:

you never really belonged to me.
you were never really mine.
from before i was walking
steady; you were walking
double time

(and never to be caught – not now).

THEATRE ANNOUNCEMENT

We ask you to remain in the bar.

The play will not go on. I think
we all knew it would end this way
but we do ask you to stay here drinking.
Drink. Drink. Be our wake. Discuss us
like we are already dead. We are in fact,
already dead. We died in tech. Our death
was cued up (but then missed). This is not true.
This is art. Art is dead. This is art.

We are dead.

My city forever birlin with my ghosts; at that corner, up that
close, outside her door, I will see my father again

heading for the water of leith,
bounding up the road; a daughter at the edge
of her father's maze, picks up
the golden thread . . .

THEATRE ANNOUNCEMENT

As a white woman I understand
I cannot possibly understand
your experience.

*Is it your 'liberalism' that leaves us
so untranslatable?*

(is what we do not ask her).

But this is not the history they want from me. the mixed-race conundrum: which story should i tell? which story should i choose?

if choice was a thing
it would be a grandmother's
ruby ring threaded with jute
cord hung around our necks

saturday, meet you by the fraser's clock?

    we'll go to the gardens to feed the squirrels
monkey nuts that we'll get from the ice-cream van . . .
    on the bus. top deck. front seats. faces pressed up to the glass
    (and once all the way to burntisland
for the fair).
    easter egg roll at silverknowes. mass at muirhouse. messages
from the shops at drylaw . . .
    at the royal infirmary, your laugh coming up the steps to meet
me as i bounded down to you in surgical supplies.
    hiding behind you at clan-like gatherings. banging pots with
you in our kitchen band . . .
    on your lap giggling as you powder puff talc between my toes.
    musical statues to the sound of the broom, banging on the
ceiling below . . .
    early mornings, in my nightie, watching you armour yourself in
your make up and heels.
    on our knees in front of the priest. at your feet feasting on
shortbread. at your table hungry fur khow . . .
    refugee camp, mythical land. *here be dragons*. survivalist fairy
tale. passed down resilience. war turned bedtime story. the trauma
inheritance. kiss before lights out. head to toe with a visiting
sister . . .
    coming sleepy off the number 32 to sprinting two at a time . . .
tap on high window still has me looking up for you. hand raised.
waving goodbye like an instinct . . .

                      watching the fireworks
                      over edinburgh castle
                      light up the back room.

THEATRE ANNOUNCEMENT

Do not make us feel uncomfortable.
Remember we came here. We paid.

It is important that the character is mixed-race
(that her story is—)

1.
i see it in a tweet
don't get me started
on all this mixed race

erasure it says.
i like it immediately
then unlike it.

(i don't know why)

to be honest, too
provocative?

2.
find myself
pulling out my phone,
to scroll through

photos of my family
for—

The (only) Power (is) in Leaving

she was told she was
a faint breeze, only echoes
quietly she goes . . .

Outside. Queuing along their gradient. She smoothes
down her hair. Later. Alone. When the party is in full
swing. She thinks. If choice was a thing . . . (I would
not have submitted to this . . .). Later. Still. With a
sudden clarity. She gets her coat;

>   (at the next head count they will re-label
>   her *the problem*; scanning the crowd . . .)

that learnt dance.

THEATRE ANNOUNCEMENT

I can't believe this is still happening,
opening her laptop, to show
everyone her seven-point plan.

Seeking Clarification

Engendering
Disappointment
Institutionally

Whit's Fur Ye'll No Go By Ye

it's aye meagre mantra,
just. crumbs. it's fur the birds.

THEATRE ANNOUNCEMENT

include some joy,
we would suggest
a dance number.

o my half-caste queen

fuckin like the starved:
discarded cloathes
on flairs of places

you didnae ask fur,
that ye came tae in
wi his breath

aw heavy haar.
o my mongrel minx,
wi yer heartbreak

ballads crooned oot
in closes. may ye rise
on a danceflair

of yer own makin,
may ye seek out
the whirlin moths,

wi wingspan
like yer own. may
ye dance,

may ye dance
wildly ...

He Died on St Andrews Day

my father & this man.
   i learnt about him from all their half rememberings.
his name uttered in incantation by drinking pals:
   The Hero of the Red Clydeside.
for my father a procession of the wounded followed
him to his grave.
   in crematorium his children stood by
him in exile . . .
   a piper played the haar in . . .
in unison *we sang, we sang* . . .
   in murmuration: *fleeting congregation.*

The Good Nurse Dance

He led the samba into the grounds. Visitor chairs as goalposts. Keepy uppy to the beat of a shift . . .

Turned them at night. Treated their sores. Charted his decline.

Washed their bodies. Laid out his days. Sung the bass line.

Made the student nurse cum in the sluice before tea.

Hid the *Racing Post* in his *Nursing Times*; kept a book for the porters . . .

Made a curry for the picket (left them the pot) back in through the morgue.

Lunch hour extended for placing the bet; for returning another lover (to her runaway life . . .)

& while the rats ran the rat runs through sedated wards he pulled the bars from the windows. To see the moon . . . Because he needed the light; the possibility . . .

(because what else did he have but flight).

THEATRE ANNOUNCEMENT

This show carries no trigger warnings.
This show carries only trigger warnings.

This show will be a series of triggers.
This show will be nothing but warnings.

This show is no longer running.
This show has exhausted us all.

This is a warning.
This is the show.

Golliwog at the Museum of Childhood, Edinburgh, 2024

we knew you were there,
had been told. forewarned.

stood in front of you, ready, set,
go for starting gun. seeing

you there, at the end of the rows
of white porcelain dolls, pretty

with perfect bows. Something
resonated: your oddity. Shared

that look of recognition, like the one
i found in the faces of aunties

as a child (oddity)
in white city.

That night, I dreamt there was a rabid dog outside our
house. I put my children behind me. But the dog finds his
way in. Had I not closed the door? I wake up in the dark.
Walk our home for hours; the poorly-paid patrol, searching
the night for dawn

i hear my boy whine
at the back door, i bring him
into me. head low. thin body shakes.

an attack dog prowls the garden,
holds a hockey stick between its teeth,
barks out *racial slurs* between the blows.

knocking the heads off our bowing tulips . . .
you bury yourself. wince as my hands fall
to you; as i sing *you're safe* in remembered melody.

the rabid dog has found his way
in through the mouse hole (that we thought
we had filled). we barricaded ourselves

in the attic (hoping he will soon
grow bored). *take our cold dinner.*
leave us (to the starving silence).

THEATRE ANNOUNCEMENT

We want the difficult conversation
sung acapella (the budget
doesn't stretch to a band).

Four poets of colour, warm up with hot chocolate, after the Edinburgh's Black History Walk, in an Italian café* on the Royal Mile

we haud bitter sugar, let it build
tae boundless bounty behind

oor lips grown tight, made pursed
wi oor whisperings: given like a sermon

at the edge of a grand square, revelation
in the doorway of a boutique hotel. furies

which mingle now, like desperate actors
wi the euro pop beats, the joint the Polish

waitress just had in the close, we watch
oor newly found secrets rise up –

rallying tae dissipating
like a drowning

(like a childhood)

in oor leavin breaths.
take a minute to look

at oor reflection,
caught bad selfie,

in the mirrored glass
behind us.

---

*That was once St Christopher Sugar House, most probably taking its name from the island of the same name in the West Indies, now St Kitts, where a shareholder in the shop, William McDowell, had considerable plantation interests.

THEATRE ANNOUNCEMENT

We will require you all to identify yourselves
in the minority to ensure our survival.
This is art. This is art.

high hopes (the legacy)

i have built up our stories so high,
i'm vertigo at the thought of you.

On seeing the Nelcau*
in the Hunterian's Virtual Collection

He said you were evidence
of how we survived the Flood.

Fitted you into a tale
he understood.

I look at you now
(virtually on my screen)

imagine your weight
in my hands,

fill you up
with more imaginings.

Is this the way of things?
The constant transference.

Does a bowl only contain what it holds?
& what holds? & what could not be held

in his story of you? You are his evidence
we survived the End & we bring you here

to our lips, to our ears, to our eyes
on a cracked phone screen . . .

But like the conch shell: you sing
(of an old longing).

*Nelcau, an ancestral relic and ceremonial vessel from Aneityum Island, Vanuatu, in the Pacific Ocean. It was collected between 1845 and 1859 by the Rev. Dr George Turner, who served as a missionary in the South Pacific and presented his collection to the Hunterian in 1860.

THEATRE ANNOUNCEMENT

Remember art is for everyone.
Remember we are everyone.

The Specials
(Saturday School)

   it's written on your face
and while i can still read you
let me take it for you, take it out
   and leave it on the step.
here we will be home. we will open the windows
   and scream it for the neighbours to keep
or the rooks!
   aye, let them caw it out.
it's staining your boots son,
   and while i still can,
let me scrub them clean.
   soak it up, screw it up, rip it up.
leave it out on the front step for
   the foxes. we will be home here.
we will dance to The Specials in our sock feet
before we open the back door
   and yell it to the sky.
we will grow strong here.
   here, sweet boy.
its shockwaves just – see?
   we will dance to The Specials
in our sock feet,
   in the half-light, leave our dirty boots fallen
by the back door. it's written on your face
   and while i can still read it. let me whisper
our stories so they will build
   to myths and legends
for you to emerge from – whole, strong, known.
   and let's curse

through the letterbox before sticking
it shut
　　with masking tape
　　　　and let's grow strong son,
dancing to The Specials – in sock feet. in our
own half-light.

In my son's room listening to records. From Loyle Carner's
'Georgetown': John Agard's 'Half-Caste'

half-light. room
the green of an olive.
i have the taste, but for you
still bitter fruit: pushing
the needle back.

THEATRE ANNOUNCEMENT

(Shut up and eat your canapés)

Theatre is the fourth emergency service.

Is that no the coastguard?

Okay...

Theatre is the fifth emergency service.

Are we sure?

On seeing Young Fathers
at the Usher Hall, Halloween 2023

in an outfit of someone still
capable of dancin for two hours

under a cape of a crowd surfer,
over a mask of who i hoped to be,

costumes of bungee jumpers in the circle,
costumes of stilt walkers in the gods.

(pints held high, in that old
reverence: *i saw . . .*)

how we rode each wave. caught
suspended in each other,

hauding up the roof
wi oor high reachin,

dancin loons – aye but
the shore we came tae

(that nicht – thegither)

singin oot:

this is. this is.
who we fuckin are.

THEATRE ANNOUNCEMENT

We understand you have high expectations.
We understand this. We are sorry. This is art.

This is art.

ACKNOWLEDGEMENTS

Some of the poems in this collection first found life as commissions; thanks is due to Edinburgh International Festival; Pitlochry Festival Theatre; Stellar Quines; Royal Lyceum Theatre, Edinburgh; Royal Society of Edinburgh and National Theatre of Scotland; Edinburgh City Council; Edwin Morgan Trust; The John Maclean Centenary Poems: *Now's The Day, Now's The Hour*; and the Hunterian Museum, Glasgow, with special thanks going to Aiden O'Rourke; Elizabeth Newman; Caitlin Skinner; Shasta Ali; Clementine E. Burnley; Anita Mackenzie; Stewed Rhubarb; Marjorie Lotfi; Gillian Finlay; Henry Bell and Alan Riach.

This collection would not be what it is without the editorial guidance of Joelle Taylor and Edward Crossan.

Special thank you, Lisa Williams, who took me on the Black History Walk in Edinburgh and inspired the poem 'Four poets of colour, warm up with hot chocolate, after the Edinburgh's Black History Walk, in an Italian café on the Royal Mile'. You are an inspiration, Lisa. Power to you always.

Thanks to my great friend and first reader, Jim Monaghan. I am forever grateful to all my fellow poets who have offered me community and friendship, especially the Scottish BPOC Writers Network, and to all my friends and family who have cheered me on and shared with me their wisdom and solidarity.

Kids! That's me done. Adrian, fancy a walk?

WITH LOVE AND THANKS TO

Typesetter	The Foundry
Cover Design	Abigail Salvesen
Proofreader	Yasmine Foyster
Production	Laura Esslemont
Publicity and Marketing	Jan Rutherford Kathryn Haldane Jennifer Andreacchi
Events	Ellen Cranston
Sales	Laura Poynton Jamie Harris Ann Landmann Carole Hamilton
Contracts and Finance	Joanne Macleod Darina Brejtrova Gayle Monteith Huy Pham
Managing Director	Hugh Andrew

Praise for

BLOOD SALT SPRING

ONE OF THE POETRY SOCIETY BOOKS OF THE YEAR

SHORTLISTED FOR THE SALTIRE SOCIETY
SCOTTISH POETRY BOOK OF THE YEAR

'An absolutely amazing collection . . . it blew me away. It feels monumental and fleeting at the same time'
DENISE MINA

'Hannah has been crucial in carving out spaces and stages for writers of colour in Scotland, and her own debut collection is a triumph'
MICHAEL PEDERSEN

'Hannah Lavery's debut collection shows her deft ability to marry the personal with the political'
ANDRÉS N. ORDORICA

'*Blood Salt Spring* offers a personal response to wider cultural conversations from national identity to personal autonomy, divisive politics to mothering during lockdown. Its terrain is vast. Its perspective unequivocal'
THE NATIONAL

'With much of the collection written in lockdown, it's poetry that feels both of the moment while reaching out and attempting to find meaning, to move forward, and find hope'
BOOKS FROM SCOTLAND

'A terrific debut poetry collection'
BBC RADIO SCOTLAND

'Hannah Lavery stole our hearts and set our minds alight with her breath-taking pamphlets and the astonishing Lament for Sheku Bayoh – for years we've been hungry for more and now finally: *Blood Salt Spring* is HERE!'
THE LIGHTHOUSE BOOKSHOP